Flower
Swallows Sing

A North Korean Memoir in Verse

Imu Baek

Translated by
Hyongrae Kim & Siobhan Meï

 HOLLYM

Carlsbad, CA

Hollym International Corp.
www.Hollym.com
contact@hollym.com   760.814.9880

Cover and book design by Jino Lee

ISBN: 978-1-56591-381-3 (paperback)
ISBN: 978-1-56591-384-4 (ebook)

Library of Congress Control Number: 2019948202

Printed in the United States of America

Translators' Note

Baek Imu's collection of poems, *Flower Swallows Sing*, offers an intimate view of the author's life as a *kotjebi*—translated here as *flower swallow*. The etymological roots of the word *kotjebi* can be traced back to the Russian word КОЧЕВОЙ, which can loosely be translated into English as "nomadic." This loan word seems to have undergone a process of localization and taken the form of a compound word comprised of the Korean words "kot" (꽃: flower) and "jebi" (제비: swallow). It is now used to refer to North Korean orphans who roam the streets of North Korea and China, flocking from one location to another, foraging for food and searching for shelter.

This translation is the result of a collaborative effort between a native Korean speaker and a native speaker of English. This process unfurled over the course of several years from roughly 2015-2019, a period during which US-North Korean relations were once again dominating global news cycles. The colorful rhetoric about dotards and nuclear bombs exchanged between U.S. President Donald Trump and North Korean leader Kim Jong-un, are part of a larger trend in U.S. media and politics that seeks to trivialize the violence of the Kim regime. In the face of farcical commentary, it becomes all too easy to forget the harrowing tales of people like Baek, who have risked death or, worse yet, incarceration in one of North Korea's infamous gulags, in order to escape the starvation and oppression of their homeland. This translation labors to make Baek's story available to English readers and hopefully, in doing so, continues her project of denouncing the violence of fascism in all of its forms.

Hyongrae Kim
Siobhan Meï

Table of Contents

Chapter 3

Chapter 4

Chapter 5

Chapter 6

Chapter 1

The Mountains are Rebelling

lately
the mountains have been rebelling

once, they offered us
herbs and mushrooms and fruit
but the angel that once bestowed its blessings
has become a raging demon—
a ghastly thing
naked and barren

like handsome curls
lush groves
once covered the mountains
where our ancestors lie
but now they've been cut down
the roots hacked up for fire

the mountain is uneven and rough
cavities dot its face
like pockmarks
the once beautiful hills
are now a mess
a bleak deathscape

the mountains
and their spirit guardians
are filled with a terrible wrath
toward those savage and ignorant folk
who dared strip them bare

thunder and lightning descend

rain and water pour down unhindered
from the gorges and ravines
overwhelming the villages—
hundreds and thousands of homes
are swept away

across this country
floods, natural disasters
grow more frequent
the people,
already pinched for food and money,
are exhausted

the country:
its people,
mountains and rivers,
writhe in pain

Hollowness

grass roots and tree bark
when I see you I feel somber
even now, I see you and feel hollow

the people seek you out
grass roots and tree bark
three meals a day
you are our only lifeline
our lives depend on you

too precious
how could we simply call you
food
instead we should call you
life

grass roots in the fields
terribly bitter
we pull them out and eat them
tree bark in the mountains
tough
we peel it off and eat it
this is barely enough to live on

you became our food long ago
you keep starving people alive
without you,
how could we speak of life?

people wander the country
across fields
and mountains
pulling and peeling, eating everything
until the fields are empty, the mountains bald
food is so scarce

is there really
no food in my country?
millions die
because there isn't
even a sorry scrap of food

who out there
will hear this cry?

Bottomless Offering Basket

in this country
far too many
have died
their lives cut short
by hunger and cold

those who have had enough,
who try to rebel,
are snatched up and tortured:

beaten, burned, stabbed, and shot

heaven knows
how many souls
have disappeared
their eyes wide open
in despair

cursed country of death
bodies in heaps
as tall as mountains
enough to fill the sea

how many more of the wretched
must be tossed
into the bottomless offering basket
before this human tragedy ends?
before someone cries:

ENOUGH

A Year of Abundance

once again
this *magical* country
has been blessed with an abundant harvest

abundance in the mountains
abundance in the fields
abundance in the rice paddies
abundance in the streets
abundance in the households

north, south, east, and west
as far as the eye can see

last autumn
the farmers
in the fields and rice paddies
reaped an abundant harvest

but after paying
the Military Provisions
the Patriotic Provisions
not a grain of rice remained

all was taken

but what's the use of complaining
during times of such abundance?

let us reap!
let us reap!
let us reap!

be it spring, summer, autumn, or winter
the season doesn't matter
the nation's policies
are superb
and thus,
there is an abundance year round

empty corpses in the mountains
empty corpses in the fields
empty corpses in the rice paddies
empty corpses on the road
empty corpses in our homes
empty corpses at every turn

vultures, crows,
the beasts of the mountains and fields
feast on meat
on the abundance
of delicious human flesh
they chant:

we shall have our fill!
the heavens love us dearly
and have blessed us with a feast!

the beasts leap in glee
amid the abundance
giving thanks for the glorious harvest

The Final Struggle

because people couldn't bring themselves
to eat the bodies of loved ones
I heard a bright fellow offered
a clever solution

apparently he suggested:

the old man in this town
dead from hunger
and the old man from that town
dead from cold
should be traded and eaten

the baby from that house
dead from hunger
the baby from the other house
dead from disease
should also be exchanged and eaten

at first we were skeptical
later we came to believe
and accept the truth,
this cursed world being what it is

the stories continue to trickle in...

a merchant was discovered
selling the flesh of a dead flower swallow
as dog meat
I heard he will be shot
by the firing squad

every day and night
these rumors spread
tales of cannibalism
stir controversy and disgust

people are eating people
but no outcry resounds—
there is only the clicking of tongues

in this final struggle
there are no words
we consume one another
we are no longer human

Mountains

if you go to the mountains
you will find them stripped naked

the starving people have plundered
the mountains
the trees
the bark
is peeled to eat
three times a day
and all that is left
is the whiteness of the bare trunks
standing dead

after the bark is peeled away
all that is left are the white trunks
people shiver in the cold
and hack at the trees with axes,
cut through them with saws,
to avoid freezing in the dead of winter
even the roots are dug up
for firewood

the ghostly mountain stands devastated—
only scattered sockets remain

mountains have no mouths
they cannot speak
yet the mountains are the naked faces of this nation:
if you look to the mountains
you will know the lives of the people
if you look to the mountains
you will see the weary-worn lives of the people

Fields

the mountains
are naked and barren
now, the people of this nation
must turn
to the fields

the fields
are their last hope
green grass in the spring
roots in the winter

but grass and roots
are not enough
to nourish the people
thus the grassroots of this nation
wither

with a heavy heart
the field embraces them,
and feeds them,
its poor children,
thinking:

I, the Field, am the Mother of these grassroots
I will care for those who the Mountain can no longer look after

The Good Old Colonial Days

I miss the old colonial days
even though times were hard
we had food on the table
at least we didn't starve
come to think of it now

the Japanese bastards were generous

now things are worse
every day innocent people
starve or freeze to death
how could we not feel nostalgic for those days?
come to think of it,

the Japanese bastards were kind

is it not enough
that people's lives are cut short,
that they die in misery?
what's more, false charges are now pressed
by the State Political Security Department
people are disappeared—
beaten, burned, and hanged

the harassment of the wretched,
of those on the brink of death,
continues:
how will they survive these hopeless days
knowing the future
that this living hell holds?

you unyielding butchers
if you kill off people like flies
when none are left
who will you oppress?
at whom will you flash your badges?
even vampires
don't suck their victims entirely dry

you cursed demons
with you at the nation's helm
we will all end up dead
and if everyone dies
what use will the country be then?

because of our dangerous words, our reactionary stances
you jackals stare at us like prey
can you rightly deny what I say?
with every word and sentence—
I SPEAK THE TRUTH

rather than leaving the nation in your hands
we would rather invite the colonial police back,
those we drove out years ago,
we will place them where you now stand
and the people will live better lives—
at least they won't starve

the idea
that people should be given a chance to live well
has been forsaken—
the State Political Security Department
is worse than the colonial police
I miss the old colonial days

Your Grandmother Wants to Die

every day they go out to the fields
where they are worked to death
the hopeful youth have nothing to eat
in this world we live in
they collapse and die
one after the other

I'm too old to earn my own,
I might as well be a cripple,
an old thing—
I should be dead
instead I take up space
one more mouth to feed

I've lived a long time,
should I die right this moment
it wouldn't be a great loss—
I should hurry to disappear
rather than remain a burden,
a useless hag

food is scarce
and the only good deed I can do,
that I must do,
for my starving loved ones
is to lighten the burden
and slip away

this way
some rice can be saved
so that my sons, daughters, and their children
can have a future
I can save them

I may be old
but I will not weigh this family down
if one of us has to die
it should be me
this ghostly old woman
should not be the reason
the precious young die of starvation

her mind is made
hot tears flow
from her caved eyes

she wraps a rope 'round her neck
and hangs herself
from the cross beam ceiling

A Cat's Complaints

the stingy people
of this household
stopped feeding me awhile back
and now
they're trying to steal *my* food

whenever they see a rat hole
they set traps
they use pickaxes and sticks to scare them out
they build fires to smoke them out
they pour in water to wash them out

nothing is left for me

I meow at them in protest
and they say:

it's too much work to catch a rat
this cat is so much bigger

I take off in haste
away from the village of people
trying to eat me
to live in the mountains, feral

Panicked Rats

the cats are gone
the hungry people
ate them all

now the world is ours
let us sing and dance

but suddenly
things take a turn for the worse:
the starving masses
have turned into cats,
their feline eyes
are narrowed
we are the ones
they are trying to catch

how did it come to this?

it was better under the Japanese,
at least we had food on the table.
now we starve to death

the elderly mutter
these risky words
when they think no one is listening

you got that right
we were better off
when it was only the cats
who were on the prowl
not these feline people

Sheep

during the day

they are herded
to a thin strip of land
with only grass to nibble on

at night

they are fenced in
no room to roam,
silenced by their fear

sometimes
they are beaten,
wounded
in the end
they will be butchered
their hides tanned
and flesh eaten

still
they are of a gentle disposition.
accepting of their fate,
they endure it all
without so much as a peep

they suffer
under their wicked and greedy owners
loyal to a fault—
they don't make the slightest attempt
to cheat their masters
pitiful and despondent,
they live like fools

my eyes brim with tears
at this sight—
I want to take you up in my arms
you so resemble
my people

those who live off of the grass
and dwell in tiny cages
victims of random acts of violence
those who offer up
silent prayers
for their nation
as blood drains from their bodies

the people are sheep
the sheep are my people

Oxen

worked to the bone
all year long
forced to toil and labor
drawing the cart without complaint
and prodded to make haste

you overworked people

rice is thrown sparingly into your troughs—
you're fed nothing but grass
yet you lower your heads
to the ground
with no sound of protest

you docile people

despite the blows of the whip
and terrible mistreatment
your mouths are still too kind
to bite your masters

Mooooo

a singular wail
not a word of dissent
or a hint of defiance

you gentle people

after all is said and done
they will use your hide
to make leather shoes
they will strip off your skin
and eat your flesh
your bones will be brewed for broth

red drops of blood will fall
from your compassionate eyes
big and protruding,
still hoping against all odds
for mercy
perhaps they will let you live?

you kind people

by the time it dawns on you
it's too late
you realize you are not people
but cattle
born into a pathetic state
victims of a sad fate

you sorry oxen

Raising a Piglet

around these parts
the richest family
owns a glorious treasure,
the envy of many,
a piglet

people whisper:

how rich you must be
to afford such a thing
there's hardly enough food around for people—
what could they possibly be feeding that piglet?

I heard
that even in that rich house
there's only one rice pot
where, then, do they cook
the pig wash?

one day
I take a peek
during feeding time
and oh my—
now I know
fresh feces from the outhouse
that's what the little piggy eats

Tailless Oxen

just like oxen
who spend all their days
toiling under the yoke,
the farmers collapse
bone tired
from the labor they are forced to do
daily

what are they
if not tailless oxen,
cows who can speak?

they have more work to do than cows,
their backs bent
from working through the four seasons,
spreading muck in the fields,
tilling the land,
seeding,
weeding,
and in the fall,
threshing

whether in the fields
or the rice paddies
no matter the type of harvest
the sweet corn,
the glutinous rice,
is claimed by the government
cornstalks and rice hulls
are all that remain
for the cowed farmers to eat

the farmers plod the mountains and fields,
in search of tree bark and grass roots
without these,
they would starve to death

these farmers:
lonelier and hungrier than bovine beasts

Better a Cow than a Farmer

cows and farmers are almost the same
but not quite
the cows fair better than the farmers
who live such pitiful lives

even though cows are worked into the ground
the government would never let
a cow die from hunger—
they are valuable laborers,
doing the work of tractors and cars

farmers however
clasp at their empty bellies
as they curl up and die,
their corpses are stacked upon one another
their lives are worth less than a cow's

a cow will not freeze to death—
it is protected from the blistering cold
by its fur coat
it can endure winter
without much discomfort

the farmer however
has no firewood to keep him warm.
the mountains have been stripped bare,
and at the height of winter
death comes in the form of cold rather than hunger

death from cold
death from hunger
how many more need to die?
there is no end to this atrocity in sight

all year long they work for this nation
they toil like cows
but are treated worse than the beasts themselves
even the cows seem surprised,
that a farmer is worth less
than one of their own at half-price

this sight
brings tears to my eyes
I can't hide or hinder
this free flowing river

you who have died with your eyes wide open,
if there is an afterlife,
if you are reborn in this country,
my advice is:
come back as a cow not as a farmer

Blessed in White

for generations now
we have been blessed by
the Great Leader,
the Eternal General,
the Supreme Commander

in both life and death,
we are blessed
we dress in white,
for we are a pure people

people starve
every day
and we wear white
to the funerals
for we are a people blessed by the heavens

blessings cascade upon us
they flow as if from a waterfall—
so many have died,
that soon there is nothing clean to wear
to the funerals,
so people paint their tattered black rags
white

yes, we are blessed
with glorious leaders
and with pure white

the starving masses,
are stretched thin like rags—
blessings,
white
clothes the nation

some blessed people
continue living—
death avoids them
for a year or perhaps a thousand,
we will bask in these blessings

please, no more of this sort of blessing—
we've had enough,
stop this offering

you swine,
you cold blooded cannibals,
you cruel dictators

Dead Nation

wherever you turn
this country
brims with death

they die here,
they die there

they die from hunger,
they die from cold

and if that wasn't enough,
they are captured,
tortured,
beaten to death,
burned to death,
stabbed to death

and if that doesn't do the trick,
they are marched in front of a crowd
to die by
firing squad,
noose,
or stake

living
is so hard
death, on the other hand,
comes easily
funeral processions
fill the streets,
while smoke continues to rise
from the tall chimneys of the crematorium

you helpless people,
before you die,
hear my bellow
shake the earth and sky!
hear me shriek
as my blood boils—
realize that you must rise!

if you must die in this devilish nation
do not do so waiting in line—
stand up for life,
rise up, unafraid!
like the mountains, arise—
overthrow this dead nation
and make it a land for the living!

Inequality

noses pierced by a metal wire
they shoulder a heavy yoke,
forced to till the earth
and savagely prodded onward

out of fear
that the cow might eat
some of the grain it has helped to grow
not only are their noses pierced with wire,
but their mouths are muzzled

the master is
miserly
sly
tenaciously brutal
and endlessly greedy
his cow is but skin and bones

the only effort
the greedy master makes
is when he tortures the poor cow
all year long the beast farms the land,
relentlessly it toils
cursed and scolded
to work faster
to do more
whipped mercilessly,
treated miserably

when autumn finally comes
the master steals
the plentiful harvest
from the paddies and fields
rice and corn
all go to his belly
and all that is left for the cow
are rice hulls and corn stalks

Path of Light

ragged clothing, empty bellies
freedoms crushed, rights stolen.
obedient as sheep, they accept their fate—
the lives that have been laid out before them

in this ghastly nation,
don't live arduously
instead, embrace death!

death is the only path
that will guide you to liberation
freedom!
happiness!

if for some reason,
you can't bear the idea
of leaving this world,
go and stare death in the eye:
rise up against tyranny,
revolt!

this is the path
that leads to survival—
a single sliver of dawn's light
to cleanse this darkness
this path of light
leads to new mornings

my ragged and hungry brethren in the north,
my 24,000,000 countrymen,
even if we die
a hundred-billion times over—
let us lay down our lives,
to hasten the coming of justice,
the path of hope,
the road to revolution!

Chapter 2

The Child Who Couldn't Close His Eyes

Halt!

a command echoes.
a child scrambles
out of a corn field

Bang!

a sharp blast of gun fire,
the running child falls
flat on his face

the child's eyes continue to stare,
in his hands
is an ear of corn,
warmed by his grasp.

that ear of corn
would've saved
his mother
and sister—
a glimmering sliver of hope
for his family's survival

even in death
the child refuses
to let go of the ear of corn

is this why his eyes remain open?

Tears

Papa was caught and shot
for stealing a sack of rice
from the storage house
one famished night

Mama starved to death
'cause she wouldn't eat her bowl
of grass porridge
in order to keep the two of us alive

Big Sister went out to beg,
going from town to town
she says she is now the mother
of our sad little hovel

no matter how long I wait
or how loudly I cry
she doesn't return

how could I have known
that on her way home,
she fell down and never got up
Big Sister froze to death
barefoot and empty-handed

Pick-Pocket

lightning fast,
a loaf of bread
is snatched up
in the marketplace

the beggar-child
gobbles, chews, and swallows
her prize while scrambling away

massive hands shoot out
grab the swallow's neck
lifting her up
by the nape

punches and kicks
rain down
a nose is bloodied,
a forehead trickles,
bodies roll in the street

I'm alive!

the child basks in this discovery
and continues to eat—
a thin smile spreading across her face

The Crime of Being Born in North Korea

hey mister, please don't hit me,
I know stealing's a crime,
but please listen

I'm a nine-year-old orphan,
I haven't committed no crime—
flower swallows are innocent!

if I must admit to a crime
there's only one that comes to mind:
I was born in North Korea

I tried to survive by begging,
but everyone's so poor
and there's no food to be had

I tried to resist,
but if stealing to live is a sin,
then I was born into a life of crime

if I could survive
by begging on the streets
I wouldn't be picking any pockets

if I'd come into this world
anywhere else but North Korea
I wouldn't be a thief
I wouldn't get caught stealing
I wouldn't be beaten
I wouldn't cry in shame

being born in this country
has made me a criminal,
so please have pity
and just this once
forgive me

Please

'scuse me ma'am,
you with the grain bag,
please stop and look at me

if you give me a kernel of corn,
I'll open my eyes,
and utter a few words

if you give me two kernels of corn,
I'll pull myself up
from where I lay

if you give me three kernels of corn,
I'll gather my strength,
and maybe I could even walk down this road

you know what, kind lady?
if you give me an entire ear of corn
a miracle will happen
right in front of your eyes:

I'll hold the corn to my heart,
and cross the Tuman River in a heartbeat—
off to find my mother in China
who left in search of food

but lady, you should know,
if you don't give me anything
I will be meeting my father
who waits for me in heaven

Food

close to death
after five days without food,
his young sibling
is the only other one left

using his last bit of strength,
the famished little boy
picks himself up
and staggers out the door

he leaves his skeletal brother
at home alone lying on the floor,
eyes closed, too hungry to cry,
resigned to his fate

on his knees,
the boy crawls and crawls
over the mountains and fields
and like a flash of light
a bit of food catches his eye:

the bark of a tree stem in the mountains,
a handful of grass roots in the fields

will this precious food
help me save my brother?

a well of hope surges up within him,
strength bursts in his body

Sweet Dreams

while we were curled up
fighting pangs of hunger,
Cheoli told us a strange story
apparently he had met a kind-hearted soul
who, for the past two days,
had fed him rice as white as snow

we stared at one another
dumbfounded
our heads shook in disbelief
starvation had finally caused Cheoli
to lose his mind

Cheoli
leaned against the wall
his eyes closed
and though exhausted,
he stubbornly insisted:

I swear it's the truth!

in his dreams, every night
he's been eating bowls of white rice

how great that must be!
even if it's just a dream
at least he's been eating
I haven't been nearly as lucky
if only I could have
such sweet dreams

we looked at Cheoli with envy
and closed our eyes
as we tried to fall asleep,
hoping we too
might dream such sweet dreams

Hogwash

Dolhe
is full of hot air again,
tooting his own horn,
telling us that
he's been eating three meals
of rice a day

the children aren't sure
how to respond to this hogwash
they grimace and smack their lips,
clutching their bellies with laughter
as tears flow down their cheeks

everyone is so poor
even grass porridge is hard to come by
who could possibly spare enough rice
to feed a flower swallow
who isn't their own child?

maybe just maybe
your story could be true
if it was just one meal—
but three meals of white rice you say?
what hogwash,
we see right through you

Are You Alive?

each morning
the first to wake
calls out
to check that none have died,

are you alive?

crawling out,
disheveled,
from a mound of dirty hay
Cheoli mutters

I am alive!

from the long shadow
of a cement wall,
eyes struggling to open,
Yongho mumbles

I did not die!

sometimes
no matter how loud we shout,
there is no answer
we tiptoe over,
shake the child,
but their body is cold
and stiff as stone

on these days
we are too sad to beg
instead, the day is spent
by our dead brother
hands clasped in prayer

this morning,
like all the others,
another fearful cry
will echo
in the still

are you alive?

Have You Eaten?

a flower swallow from Wonsan greets me,

have you eaten today?

I tilt my head in response
and think for a moment

did I eat today or not?
I wrack my brain
and scratch my head
then I slap my knee—that's right!

this morning I dug up a bit of savory corn
from a cow patty

I have eaten today!

Riddle

their leader gathered
the flower swallows in a huddle
and told them this riddle:

I am a bird but I cannot fly
what kind of bird am I?

a sly child cries:
a chicken!

but another has the better answer:
a flower swallow!
look at us, we can't fly!

this earns the child a pat on the head:
you really are a bright one!

the older boy closes his eyes, wracks his brain,
and comes up with another question:
which country in the wide-wide-world
has the most flower swallows, do you reckon?

the flower swallows tilt their heads
and shout out in unison:
North Korea!

the child elder asks:
and the poorest?

the young ones cry:
the flower swallows of North Korea

the king of the flower swallows beams with pride
as he lets out a chuckle:

you are certainly the brightest
group of flower swallows to wander this world

now take flight!
gather what you can
and don't get caught!

Holiday Spread

eat your fill!
flower swallows gather round a large rock, their table,
eager to present what they have brought
to the holiday feast

Cheoli stole a few kernels of corn—Grain
Younghee, the beggar,
brought a few dried radish leaves—Greens
Hoonhee gathered several silk worms—Meat

a rare and delectable holiday spread

Doli picked some wild pears from the mountain.
they're bitter because they're not in season,
but beggars can't be choosers
after all they're good enough to eat

Yongsu caught a crawfish in the river—
only one so there's not much to go around,
but roast it on the fire and everyone can have a taste
of this delicacy

Okhee came across a bit of bone at a restaurant
it's so hard, it cracks our teeth,
but times are tough,
and every last bit of marrow is precious,
so of course all will be consumed

those of you who have come empty handed:
there's no need to be shy!
gather 'round and be merry,
happy holidays to all!

the feast is soon over
yet bellies still growl in hunger
but we are gathered 'round a table together—
isn't that what the holidays are all about?

Hibernation

listen up!

this winter night is so cold
that we can hear the birch tree cracking—
we must huddle together

among the flower swallows gathered here,
the child from Hamhung is no more than a baby
barely four years old,
if we aren't careful he might freeze to death
place him in the middle,
the older children will form a tight circle
around him like an oven

wait!

I almost forgot her—
the only girl among us,
weaker than most,
she's someone we should protect
she'll sleep in the middle
make sure the warmth doesn't seep out,
pack your bodies together tightly

listen up!

it's a cold, bitter winter night,
enough to make the foxes cry,
let us pray to the earth and sky
that we may survive the night

Food for Flower Swallows

when there's nothing left to steal
and the people are too poor to beg from
flower swallows have a way of making ends meet

flower swallows aren't particular
they'll eat grass from the fields
flowers from the hills

talented they are, these flower swallows
they munch on dragonflies
and snack on tired butterflies

leaping grasshoppers and jumping frogs
dead snakes, sickly rats, chirping chicks
all can be eaten

Nature, the world's largest restaurant,
has plenty of food for swallows
so this is where they set their table

Communism's Bounty

there is a garbage dump
behind the luxurious apartment complex
where the powerful
party members reside

in this dump you can find
mouth-watering fish bones
tasty radish skins
fragrant apple cores
your heart's desire

hardened rice cake
snacks covered in fungi
some spoiled rice
all these delicacies
from the mountains and the seas
make for a sumptuous feast

with nowhere else to turn
and no one to lean on
we're always grateful
for this Communist supermarket
that we shop through every day

in it
you can find all you'd ever want
torn cotton clothes
tired socks
discarded shoes
find it and it's yours
free of charge

they may not have a penny between them
but the flower swallows are excited
gathering, sharing their findings
there is no yours or mine
in this Communist goldmine

when I was young
I'd wear my necktie
and pledge allegiance
to Communism
this dream we all admired
and here find ourselves
amid its bounty

Young Criminals

we're happy!

they tell us we're a disgrace
to this nation,
this socialist paradise
which is supposed to be
full of happy children

one day in his car
the General said:
pickpockets!
vagrants!
these children need to be locked up!

and so they built
Children's Camp 2.13

according to a special state decree
hundreds of beggar children
from all corners of the nation
were rounded up

among them
a two year old flower swallow
whose mama and papa died from hunger

this baby,
the littlest of the young criminals,
was given special treatment
by the care mothers

when the babe whined,
or cried from the heat of a fever
they would feed it a mysterious pill every couple of days

when the child wept for food
they cursed
and fed it a flower
when the older children
were beaten to death with the rod
the baby's punishment was light
if it cried for its mama and papa
it was locked up for four days without food
until it stopped wailing

devotion will make flowers blossom from stones
maybe the people of this nation
weren't devoted enough
to merit the shining rays of the General's grace

within a month of its arrival
that whiny baby flower swallow,
the youngest criminal,
who was always crying
for its mama and papa in heaven,
flew up to meet them

you might not be dressed in prison garb
but you're all little jailbirds
in this children's prison camp

you lazy bums,
with your impure thoughts
you have committed so many crimes
at such a young age

instead of being pious children,
loyal subjects,
you starved and begged
and became disrupters of the great socialist system

you stand accused
for betraying the nation
with your begging
for pickpocketing
because you were hungry
for stealing from the people
you thieving brats

the nation is in crisis
there are no handouts
especially for the offspring of lowlifes
who have no relation to the leaders of the revolution

tsk tsk tsk
we rounded your lot up
to work in the labor camps
but you're all so small and weak
the slightest breeze sends you reeling,
knocks you down
and you never get back up

you immature pathetic little things
you good for nothings
are a burden to the country
a headache

we don't have cloth
to make you uniforms
it would be a waste anyway—
work as you are
then die

maybe, for you lot,
death might be better
than starving every day
to be worked to the bone
and endure beatings

oh, by the endless grace of the great General—
who stands taller than the sky—
the king of this nation,
bestows unto you
a final blessing

Chapter 3

Milk

from lack of food
her breasts are empty
yet the baby gropes
at her barren bosom
and cries out
eunga eunga

the mother's tears
flow
as she clutches
her wretched baby
crying from hunger

her baby begins to
frantically
suckle
on her salty tears
chok chok
as if they were milk

Baby's Bowl

poor family
the baby's only meal
is its mother's milk

its mother's breasts
are the baby's bowl—

but all that remains
in this meager bowl
are bones
not a grain of rice to behold

lying face down,
the hungry child
holds the bowl to its mouth
and cries all day long

ten days later,
no longer able to bear the sight
of her crying child,
the mother dies

cold hearted people—
they carry away the child's hopes,
its empty bowl

Wordless

clutching her child
the mother
dies
on her back
eyes wide open

even in the end
she could not bear to close them

against her chest
the baby
gropes at barren breasts
and dies
mouth to nipple

people pass
and turn their heads
to ignore
the sight of
two empty corpses

Baby's Wish

no mama
no papa
baby is left alone
in the empty hovel

mama
starved herself
to feed her child

papa
well, he wouldn't eat either

they endured without food
and went to heaven

but what's a baby to do
without its mama and papa
to hold it close?

the baby is all alone
cold and hungry—
lonely during the day
afraid in the night

the baby wonders
if I starve
will I follow my mama and papa
to heaven?

without my mama and papa
I don't care to live in this world
I don't want to be alone anymore

let me be with my mama and papa

Thinking About Mama

did she run off
because I nagged her
by asking for food?

she used to hold me in her arms
and shed tears
while she comforted me

my poor mama was also hungry
she was probably sick of me
she must've hated me in the end

one day without a word
she left for a better place
with no promise of return

mama, come back
I won't be such a pest
I promise not to be a nuisance

I miss you so—
if you come back
I will gladly starve in your arms
and happily die in your embrace

In That Place

my papa's emaciated face
appears in my dreams:
why are you so thin?
I thought there was no such thing as hunger in that place

my mama's shaky hands
appear in my dreams:
why are you so cold?
I thought there was no winter in that place

why is there no rice in that place?
are the people hungry?
does the snow fall cold and heavy
where my mama and papa are?

maybe this is why
mama and papa
haven't come back for me
and I only see them in my dreams

Dream

last night
I saw my mama
her mouth was dry and quivering
as she tried to feed me a spoonful of grass porridge

last night
I saw my papa
he tried to hold me in his arms
as he caressed me with his bony hands

last night
I was so happy in my dreams
though I was hungry
I was with my mama and papa
and my heart swelled with joy

mama and papa
where did you go?
why did you abandon me here?

I clutch
at their necks
I whine
I cry

mama!
papa!
I choke on my screams
and wake up

mama
nowhere to be found
papa
nowhere to be seen

all that is left
are the snowflakes slowly falling on my cheeks
blessings from mama and papa
a warm embrace

Letter to Heaven

they must be in heaven,
my mama and papa

they were kind people
who lived like angels
before they perished
they must've gone to heaven

I asked the neighbor's daughter
to write them a letter
on the envelope she wrote their name and address:

>   Soonhee's
>   Parents Heaven

the mailman said
he couldn't take my letter
because I didn't have a stamp

please, sir
I've got no money for stamps
please, could you just take my letter?

Happiness

if tonight
I dream
first
I'd like to
see my mama

if tonight
I dream
I'd also like
to eat a bowl of white rice

I'd like to eat
a bowl of rice
cooked by
my mama
as if she'd never gone away

Little Mother

papa
he starved to death long ago
and today
mama has left us as well
what do we do?

my poor siblings
don't you cry
from now on
I'll be your mother

I may be small
but I'm still bigger than you
I'll be your little mother
I'll carry you on my back
and feed you

before our mama
closed her eyes
she asked me
to be your new mother

so from now on
whether we beg or steal
we'll stick together
steadfast
strong

A Flower Swallow's Birthday Wish

yesterday
I wanted a bowl
of my mama's grass porridge

today
a bit of radish peel
from the garbage dump
is my wish

tomorrow
I hope to die quickly
so I can meet
mama and papa in heaven

Birthday Party

if someone
were to throw me a birthday party
I'd like rice and water

I'd scoop
mounds of white rice into a bowl
with a spoon made of bronze
and I'd add a bit of water
to wash it all down

and if that person
were so nice
as to grant me another kindness
I would ask
for a bit of soy sauce

if you add a spoonful of sauce
to the water
it might as well be soup
I can't think of anything better
than rice and soup

Wish

down from the sky
fluffy white snow falls

if it was rice—

the hungry children of this country
would never ever starve to death

down from the sky
wooly white snow falls

if it was cotton—

the ragged children of this country
would never ever freeze to death

Tiny Egg

chirp chirp!
goes the barn swallow
as she lays a little egg in her nest
under the eaves of the house—
a precious tiny thing

but where did it go?

the hungry child of the house
climbed a ladder to the nest
high in the beams
where no one could reach
and stole it

cluck cluck!
went the hen
they wrung her neck a while back
now the chicken coop is empty
there are no more delicious eggs to boil

soon after
from south of the river
this barn swallow flew in
and laid an egg in her nest
under the eaves

heh heh!
the babe saw it there
and clapping its hands in delight,
exclaimed:
the bird laid a tiny egg!

the sight of the tiny warm egg
made the child's mouth water
clenching the egg
in its sweet little hands
the child came down the ladder
and dropped the egg
into a pot of boiling water
then swallowed it whole
without peeling off the shell

Apple Pride

I ate an apple today—
bet you wish you were me!
Na-nana-naa-nah!

what?
you had an apple?
how? where?
perhaps one of us has seen an apple
but surely no one has ever eaten one
stop your silly lies!

I'm not lying!
let me tell you how it happened,

I was really lucky!
today at the garbage dump
I spied a pretty little plastic bag
and in it, the peel and core of an apple
and I scarfed the whole thing down

Memories and Old Lies

what memories of North Korea
haunt you the most?

I'll never forget
being so hungry
it brought you to tears
being so weak
the wind could topple you over

what memories of China
will stay with you forever?

I'll never forget
holding my breath
ears pricked up
stomach churning
in fear of being captured

what lies were you told
that you might divulge
many years from now
when the nation is reunited?

we used to cry
for the South Korean children
who had to
beg for their dinner

that lie will be forgotten

Chapter 4

Final Prayer

O Lord

I kneel before you
my eyes closed
my hands clasped
before I die
from cold or hunger,
please hear my prayer:

I am a flower swallow
hungry and dressed in rags
my parents, brothers and sisters
have all perished
if I were to disappear from this world too
no one would notice or care
I am as worthless as an insect

if there is a life hereafter,
if I am to be born once more,
O Lord,
let me be born in any other nation
than North Korea

please let it be any country
in the deserts of Africa
or even the freezing tundra of the North Pole
anywhere else but here

my life has been one of misfortune
due to a sin I did not commit
the sin of being born in North Korea
I have been treated
with disdain and contempt
and now, at last, I will meet my end

all I ask of you
as your lowly servant
is that I may be reborn in a different nation
and grow up treasured,
I only ask that I may live a happy, decent life
and close my eyes peacefully
when my time comes

O Lord,
if there is a life after this one
for this poor orphan,
whose wearisome existence
has been cut short by tragedy,
please grant this final prayer
offered up in tears

Child's Responsibility

younger me
wanted to live virtuously
but looking back
over my short life
I see I have committed too many sins

mama and papa
who loved me so
starved to death
because I slurped down
the last bit of grass porridge

I moved around the country
as a flower swallow
stealing food
because I was hungry
and making off with people's laundry
because I was cold

even worse
I betrayed my homeland,
the one that birthed and raised me
I fled to a different country
where I roamed about with an empty belly
begging for a living
a traitor
a sympathizer
a disgrace to my nation

sins I committed on purpose
and sins I committed unknowingly
countless misdeeds
carried out in moments of weakness
sins so numerous
if stacked up they'd reach the sky

just as the tortoise struggles under his heavy burden
my shoulders bend under the weight of my crimes
if I die
I'm surely destined for eternal damnation
please, O merciful God,
don't let me fall into that fiery pit
if I must go
please send me to heaven
to my mama and papa
whom I dearly miss

though I'm only twelve years old
I have committed many sins
I don't yet have the wisdom
to understand this dark world
I am pathetic, a child

please take these circumstances
into consideration
have pity on me
the day I die

if I am to be punished
please let it not be too harsh
please don't send me to hell
O merciful Father in heaven

Liberation

friends,
the hour of death is near!

hear my words:

whether by hunger or cold
soon we will be liberated
we will leave this hell
and be free from all manner of suffering

friends, don't look back,
wipe away your tears
shake off any regrets or fears
take hold of one another's hands
and march forward
toward our liberation

Threshold

off we go
to paradise,
leaving cold and hunger behind us

could there be a better place
for us, the ragged and starved?

heaven is where
mama and papa are
how great a place it must be

finally
our wishes have come true
we are at the gates of heaven—
we can leave our burdens behind
and walk forward together
lighthearted

Fellow Traveller

one, two, three, four, five
let's go
hand in hand
holding tight

to anyone else
death would be a lonesome affair—
a path travelled unaccompanied
but we five are not alone
we will walk that path
hands clasped tight
what good fortune

so what if
this is the last road?
it may be a ghastly way,
but we are brothers
bound together
strong and steadfast,
I am not afraid,
I feel safe

my friends,
even if this path is steep
we must have each other's back

one, two, three, four, five
let's go
hand in hand
clasped tight

North Korean Children

O Lord,
if I could make one wish
before I die
would you grant it to me?

O Lord,
I flicker like a candle flame in the wind
please listen to this dying flower swallow's
final wish!

O Lord,
I have lived my life in hell
please, now, deliver me to heaven

Heaven

my poor little sister,
we are going to die of starvation
but do not fear—
do not feel sorrow

once we die
we'll go to that place
where mama and papa are

where is this place?
anywhere we can be together
is heaven

a world
without cold or hunger
where we'll always be together
where we'll be happy forever

we will leave this weary world behind
and go to that beautiful paradise
what is there to fear?
why should we grieve?

my dear sister,
draw upon your last bit of strength
let's clap our hands
death is mercifully near—
let's greet it with a smile!

let my belly growl on even louder
let the wind blow harder and freeze my veins
so that my sister and I
may hastily arrive in heaven
where mama and papa wait for us,
waving

Hell

mama and papa
both died of hunger

I, myself a flower swallow
will soon die in this land

this nation is a living hell
filled with hungry flower swallows

the king of this nation,
Lord of the Underworld
has opened the gates
to his fiery domain

Enemy

I close my eyes
and hang myself

why go through the trouble
of living this wretched life
living one more day
means enduring more pain
death is a comfort
free from cold and hunger
what bliss

I'm nearly there—
joy is in my grasp
when suddenly
you save me

why have you come between
me and my happiness?
don't you have anything better to do?

saving me
a girl, poisoned by anger,
doesn't make you my savior—
it makes you my enemy

Impulse

how wonderful it would be
if there were no such thing
as countries—
all of the pain in this world
would evaporate

if I were to vanish,
all of the afflictions
that have ailed me since birth
would disappear

if I were to cease to exist,
I can't say for sure
if I would be happy
but at least
this pain would end

Hoon's Last Day

for several days
he had been starving,
suffering from disease—
he stuck it out for so long
but one day he told us

you all know—
you've seen how I suffer
all I can think of
is a quick end to
the hunger,
the bitter cold,
the pain,
as this disease gnaws at my bones

he could barely
lift his frozen body
he creaked forward
on all fours
like a heavy wagon
and just like that
hurled himself
over the edge of the cliff

Child's Concerns

cold, hunger, disease
are endless
how great it would be
to stop all of this pain,
to fall dead
just like that

I long for it
but I hesitate, waiver
a painful tightening
in the depths of my heart

they say it hurts horribly
to die
that the pain of it
is unfathomable
if I were to die
me, who's afraid of needles—
would I be able to bear it?
is there a way it could be less painful?

if I cannot avoid it
might there be a way
to make it quick
to reduce the agony?

I wish I could die
in a single second
that would be best
or maybe ten
at most a minute
if I'm going to die
the quicker the better

everyday I wonder
what must I do
to overcome this final obstacle?

I want to die so badly
but I am so afraid

Exactly

so, what do you think:
is it easier to live or to die?

of course it's easier to die—
'cause once you're dead
you can't feel
hungry or cold anymore

psh
in that case,
why don't you just roll over and die?

hah
if only if it were that simple

If All We Needed Was Air

how wonderful would it be,
if there was no such thing as food?
without food
we'd never go hungry
we'd never be charged with robbery

how wonderful would it be,
if I didn't have a stomach?
without a stomach
I could never be hungry

if all we needed was air,
if that was enough
how wonderful that would be—
air is so plentiful here on earth!

Last Farewells

tonight is a night of farewells
we are worn out—bone-tired from this life
this is our last day in this world,
the loneliest night

bellies stuck to our spines,
dressed in rags
the freezing wind
has made us numb
I don't think we'll survive
the night!

the blizzard has gained strength
the wind is picking up—
how will we survive
the night?

my friends,
fold your bodies in like snails
huddle together
let us drive away the cold
even if it's just for a moment—
so that we can decide
what to do in our final hours

the most important thing
is that we smile
and exchange firm handshakes
if we are to go
our last farewell should be a proper one

when we lived in this world
we always relied on one another
and overcame countless difficulties
we're as close as brothers—
on this final day
we must exchange proper goodbyes

let us
lose ourselves in the sad memories
of our lives cut short
we shared sadness and joy
let us thank one another
for our kinship
in this frightful world

now that we're about to leave behind
all those weary days
that I wanted to forget,
I grieve their passing
my tears flow
let us share these stories one last time

my brothers,
let us confess
that our hearts are full with love for one another:
that we are sources of comfort
that we live and die together

this is our last night
before we leave this world
let us hold hands
exchange farewells
shed tears
we have so many tales to tell

Thinking about My Friends

it's so hard
to live in this world
my thoughts
often turn to the world hereafter

a month ago
Cheoli died of hunger
I hope he isn't hungry anymore

a few days ago
Yonghee froze to death
I hope he's found warmth

they should both be comfortable now
in that faraway place

those who remain here
are still cold and hungry
suffering and dying

Cheoli and Yonghee
have turned their backs to this horror
I envy them

lately it's been strange—
my thoughts linger
on those two

Loyalty

should God come this evening
to take us home
let us grasp one another's hands firmly
in humble reverence
let us kneel in prayer
and, in honest faith,
make our last requests

O Lord,
should you take us,
please do not scatter us—
take us to the same place

living together in this dark world,
we shared sadness and pain
like brothers, we are bound to one another
by a fierce loyalty—
we cannot be separated

let us be together when we go,
so that whether in heaven or hell,
we may lean on one another
and be strengthened

we are a band of brothers
we cannot be divided by death
no matter where—
in this world or the next—
we pray that we remain together
O Lord, please smile down
upon our loyal friendships
and grant us this one last wish

Chapter 5

Flower Swallows and Weasels (1)

weasels reside
in hillside hollows
but flower swallows
wander the countryside

weasels crawl out
of their burrows
to steal hens and rabbits—
no one calls them criminals

but a flower swallow
caught stealing
is beaten
and sent to prison

this is the fate of flower swallows—
we will always be worse off
than weasels

Flower Swallows and Weasels (2)

weasels are wealthy—
their bellies are full,
they always have plenty

how warm they must be,
covered in thick fur
with burrows to call home

without fur
and no burrows to call home,
flower swallows blossom in the spring
only to die when the winter wind blows

the flower swallows who wander this country,
brave cold winter winds
under the eaves
of a stranger's home,
shaking and shivering
until they freeze

Swallow

swallow, swallow
what kind of swallow are you?

are you
a barn swallow
or a flower swallow?

barn swallows
have warm nests
and pretty wings
that carry them to open skies
filled with dreams

flower swallows
have no home to return to
nor wings to fly—
we wander on foot,
our dreams abandoned along the way

barn swallows
spread their wings—
when autumn winds arrive,
they are the first to find their way
to warm, abundant lands

flower swallows
are flightless birds—
we cannot cross rivers
instead we blow on our frozen hands
and jump about to stay warm

a flock of wandering swallows
who made it across the border
gather at a crossroads
as the snow falls slowly
to seek shelter for the night

Cruel Winter

weasels are born into this world
in cozy underground tunnels
wearing soft, warm coats

no matter how long the winter
they never have reason to fear the cold—
they go about their business in rich overcoats
like little lords

if only my mama and papa
had been weasels—
then I could've been their soft-coated offspring

O Lord,
if the rags on my shoulders
aren't enough this cruel winter,
in the next life
let me be born a weasel
and not a lowly flower swallow

As Luck Would Have It

it's a shame
I was born a flower swallow

instead of a tree swallow
that would have been grand

or a barn swallow
with a place to call home

even a cliff swallow
would've been nice

but as luck would have it
I came into this world
a flower swallow

A Flower Swallow's Song for Unification

I envy those swallows
who freely take flight—

those swallows
who soar through springtime skies
and fly south
when the winter cold sets in

in this nation, however,
the hungry, freezing flower swallows c
an't go south
they are a flightless flock—
their wings flap only in their dreams

the passage to
that southern land
of warmth, wealth, and kin,
is cut off by the border—
the 38th parallel

Wings Desperately Beating

flower swallows like me
dream of that country
where children live
free from cold and hunger

but the way south is blocked
none can cross
that border

yearning for escape
the choice is made
to fly northward

a lucky few
find their way
others die
from cold, violence, and hunger

flower swallows
southern dreams
wings desperately beating

The Final Will and Testament of a Flower Swallow

we are flowers:
we bloom in the spring
and in the winter,
freeze

if a flower swallow dies,
be sure to bury it
on a sunny hillside
and plant a seed on its grave

when spring arrives
a flower will bloom—
water the plant
like you would feed grass porridge to a beggar

in my gratitude
I will salute you
by dancing in the breeze
a flower
rooted firmly in the past

Don't Need 'Em

ain't no
big dishes or cabinets
in my house

don't need 'em

ain't no
bowls or tables
where I live

don't need 'em

ain't got
spoons
'cause there's no rice
in this home

don't need 'em

sold it all
to eat
but now there's nothin' left

my parents starved to death
so I left the house

that place means nothin' to me

dead broke
begging in the street—
I'm a flower swallow now

got rid of all I didn't need
all I've got left are my arms and legs—
free as a bird
I travel the world

Biggest House in the World

who would dare call me
a child beggar, a pauper,
a hobo with nowhere to call home

nonsense—
the sky is the roof over my head
and the land is the floor

if there is anyone out there
who has a bigger house than mine
come out and show yourself!

I'm a person of means,
with the biggest house in the world—
a millionaire who wants for nothing

Tastiest Food in the World

what is the
tastiest food
in the world?

the tastiest food
in the world
is crunchy roasted grasshopper

the most delicious meal
in the world
is savory boiled frog

but
when summer turns to winter
and there are no more grasshoppers or frogs
what tasty things will there be left to eat?

rat meat, of course,
dead from disease
lying by the side of the road
that's the most delicious thing in the world

Flower Swallows Everywhere

one day
all of the household pets decided to run away
because the famished villagers
wanted to slaughter them for food

the loyal ox and goat didn't make it—
neither did the foolish pigs or chickens
the rabbit thinks he's smart,
but he's too good-natured to scamper off
smart and swift, we are the only ones
to make it out of that town alive

no one else but me
a clever mutt
and you, a nimble kitty

we won't ever go home
to die like those idiots
we will live in the mountains and fields—
a wild dog and a feral cat

how are we any different from
those flower swallows?
they exist everywhere
in droves

Lucky Neighbors

I'd rather be a beggar
in a rich country
than in a poor one

even if you set out
with nothing but an empty can,
beg in a rich country
and the handouts will fill your belly

the poor people here
are skin and bone—
if they're lucky
grass porridge is their one meal of the day

people here don't have enough porridge
to fill their own bellies,
how could they possibly spare food
for us troublesome flower swallows?

simply visit the restaurants
of our rich neighbors
and your eyes will widen
at the sight of decadence

this was the first time in our lives
that our eyes feasted on such delicacies—
food from the mountains and the seas
piled so high, the table legs creaked
the guests left half of it untouched—
mounds of food forming delicious peaks

no one eats food
that's already been served
so it's thrown out with the waste
for the pigs to eat—
they call this food "leftovers"

how wonderful it must be
for the beggars of that rich nation
they can be lazy all day
and when they're hungry
simply visit a restaurant
and have their fill of leftovers

they belch and laugh
just for our benefit—
those blessed beggars
of our rich neighboring nation
how I envy them

Reincarnation

the rich pigs
across the border
eat until they're about to explode

but the poor flower swallows of this nation
die of starvation
because they lack
even a meager bowl of grass porridge

the rich pigs
across the border
each have a stay
they call home

but the poor flower swallows of this nation
are homeless
and wander aimlessly

the rich pigs
across the border
get plumper by the day

but the poor flower swallows of this nation
grow gaunt with each passing hour

the pigs across the border
are happier than us flower swallows—
I hope that in my next life
I am born a pig
so that I, too, may be happy

Traveling Abroad

the poor flower swallows of our country
invite their neighbors
from across the border
for a visit
but no matter how much they nag,
their friends never want to come

why would they bother?
we can't even offer them
a bowl of grass porridge—
they'd leave with an empty stomach

flower swallows however
don't need an invitation
every year we make the journey
to visit our rich neighbors

but when we go to visit them
we always eat our fill
and life suddenly seems
worth living again

Operation Border Crossing

no need for papers
flower swallows
prefer to travel empty handed
nimble and free

like the partisans
who lost the Japanese garrison troops
by crossing the Yalu and Tumen River
we advance across the border
by leaps and bounds

there might be guards
but we have plans to give them the slip
we look left and glance right
and shoot forward like bullets

no need for boats
in the summer we swim
in the winter we slide
across the border
there's nothing to it

we migrating birds
take flight in the spring
and return in the fall
every year we perform
operation border crossing
it's no trouble at all

Migration

even the birds
have decided to fly away in flocks

good harvest or bad,
it doesn't matter,
people are everywhere:
they hover over the grain fields
and rice paddies
like a swarm of bees

there are more people
in the fields
than there is grain to harvest—
up and down the rows they move,
stripping them bare

not an ear of rice—
not so much as a single grain remains
now the birds will starve
unless they move away

all of the sparrows are dead
they died with their voices raised
in protest

chirp chirp

now all is quiet
all the birds
have followed the flower swallows
they have flown together
across the border

Chapter 6

Neither Lords nor Flowers

we lowly children
are not the lords of this nation
we're despised—
there's nothing great about us
except that we are great beggars

with unwashed faces
and ragged clothes
we're far from being flowers—
we're flower swallows

orphans abandoned by society
neither lords nor flowers
we have no dreams
cold and hunger are our inheritance

Curious

it's a curious thing
that the flower swallows
across the border
never die from the cold,
their thick coats cover them snugly

it's a curious thing
that the swallows
across the border
scavenge enough food
that they never die from starvation

we are all poor flower swallows
so why is it
that the flower swallows of this nation
are so much poorer,
and so raggedly dressed
with growling, empty bellies?

we are all wandering flower swallows
so why is it
that the flower swallows of this nation
face a worse fate?
each night another dies
from cold
from hunger

If

the lyrics of
"The Greatest Country in the World" go:

the Kimjongilia
is the most beautiful flower
the Great Leader's statue
is the tallest
the Arch of Triumph
is the largest
the Juche Tower
is the grandest
the Mass Gymnastics Performance
is the greatest
Our Dear Leader
is supreme
the Rodong Party
is glorious
Socialism
is superior to all

so then why
if the lyrics are true
why are we so ragged?
why are we the hungriest swallows?
why are we the poorest country of all?

?

a great Supreme Leader
and
downtrodden citizens

a refined Worker's Party
and
hungry flower swallows

superior policies
and
utter human disaster

this strange country
is impossible to understand

?

a swallow nests under the eaves of a house
deep in thought

The Nation's Flowers

the benevolent leader
gave this nation's
flower buds the following blessing:

"go forth and blossom!"

however
a bud needs water
if it's going to flower
and no water has been given—
so we wither and die

we haven't been planted in pots
nor gently placed on windowsills,
we've been forced outdoors
where it does nothing but snow

how are we to blossom?

The Little Matchstick Girl

at least the little matchstick girl
had leftover matches
when it was cold,
she could strike one and feel the warmth
my hands are empty

in the tiny light of the flame
she imagined seeing cooked goose
and her grandmother approaching—
I don't have the pleasure of such hallucinations

the little matchstick girl and I
are so different:
she had goods to sell while I am a beggar
she was much better off

Orphan

"Blossom!"

"Be Joyous!"

"We Envy No One!!"

I stagger about
words on colorful posters assault my eyes—
they cover the walls
of every street and alleyway

I can't blossom—
I wither from hunger every day
my family starved to death
so now I am on my own

why can't I feel joy?
grief buries me

my heart bursts with envy
as I watch children
walking hand-in-hand
with their mothers and fathers

Wailing

I bellow at the sky
but not in anger
I thrash about on the ground
but not in madness

I have nowhere to go
under this endless sky
on this vast earth
I stare up at the clouds
and stamp my feet
shrieks and howls
escape my mouth

may the earth split
and swallow me whole—
may the sky boom
and strike me with lightning

Dawn

it was dark yesterday
it is dark today
it will be dark tomorrow

we trudge
through the dark night
but there is no end to this path
to this long, arduous march

there is no telling day from night—
for it's always as dark as midnight

darkness is before us
and behind us
darkness stretches over the mountains
and fields
in all four directions

we dare not dream
that the dazzling sun will rise,
that its rays will ever shine upon us

not even
a slice of the moon
a young little star
can be seen from the depths
of this long, dark night

all I ask
is for a strand
of faint light
to fall upon me

a hint of dawn
would be enough
to sustain me

I fear I might never see
that sliver of light

I want to walk
holding on fiercely
to the ray of hope
inside me
so that it won't be extinguished

Dreams of a Flower Swallow

flower swallows don't dream
of holding out their empty hands
and collecting alms

flower swallows dream
of handing out goods
to those in need

we are so poor and ragged
that we must wander and beg for a living
but we flower swallows have a dream—
one we keep hidden away

it's such a beautiful vision
it rises in the sky like a rainbow—
a dream
as colorful as a mirage

if one day
I own a great castle
I'll throw a party

I'll invite all of the hungry children
who wander the earth
to this great celebration

I'll sell all of my precious jewels
to clothe those poor little ones
and I'll feed them day after day
so that they no longer need to beg
and endure disdain and scorn
I'll be their benevolent king

who would dare say
that flower swallows don't dream—
our oldest dream,
our greatest wish
is to rid this world
of hunger and misery

Magic Wand

if I ever got my hands
on a magic wand
I would give it a wave
and make the world a better place

Abracadabra!
let there be rice
Abracadabra!
let there be cake
gather the nation's starving children
so they may eat their fill

Abracadabra!
let there be clothing
Abracadabra!
let there be shoes
dress them in warm outfits
so they can toss their rags away

for my final magic trick
I would bring back the mothers and fathers
of all orphaned children
so that they may be happily reunited

if I ever find a magic wand—
the one in all the fairytales—
I would give it a wave
and make this dark world
a brighter place

Remembering Father

O Lord,
my heavenly Father,

thanks to you,
I've made it this far
when there was nothing to eat
you gave me food from the sky

I survived
by drinking the summer rain
by eating from the piles of winter snow

at times,
perhaps because I had sinned,
hail would pelt down
and strike my head like tiny fists

my own dear father was an angry drunk
when it was all too much
he'd resort to rubbing alcohol
and his rage would hail down upon us

my family was so poor
sometimes we collapsed from hunger
and father would feed us
water with a pinch of salt

O Lord,
this is why
when I go to church
I call on You,
Father

Mother, in Memoriam

mother,
it was three years ago today
that you died of starvation
my heart sinks as I think of you

all I have to place on this boulder
which serves as an altar
to your memory,
is a handful of grass, fit for a goat
I have nothing else to offer
for I am homeless and wander about

mother
don't reprimand me
this is the best food I could find
the grass is a bit withered because it's winter
but it's all I could manage

so don't be angry
this is the best I could do
as your only son left in this world
please accept these offerings
at the table I have set
because I miss you,
my dear and loving mother

when you were alive
you gave me all of your love
with every spoonful of grass porridge
you fed me
until the day you collapsed,
you called me the apple of your eye

mother,
I had no idea
I was a foolish child,
who starved his mother to death
only now do I understand
your boundless love
today I bellow and wail
and beg your forgiveness

mother,
I've grown since you last saw me
no need to worry
I clasp my hands together in prayer—
please accept this offering
and rest in peace

Letter to God

dear Lord,
I write to you from my home—
it's snowing heavily now

the sky above my head
is the ceiling
the ground on which I lie
is my bed

this branch is my pen
which I use to write
upon this sheet of white
that covers the ground

how are my mother and father
who have returned to your embrace?
do they ever cry
because they miss the child
they left behind?

dear Lord,
tell my father and mother
that I am well
that I have been eating my fill
since I came to this country
that I am dressed in warm cotton clothing
they needn't worry about me

do my father and mother
worry that the child they left behind
has fallen terribly ill
from these chilly winter nights?

father and mother
you should stop worrying!
if one day
I should finally become fatally ill,
a blessing I hope for,
this will mean that I will soon be at your side
a cause for celebration

dear Lord,
if you were to call me home,
I would leave the heavy burden of this life behind,
and come running,
to meet my father and mother
heart fluttering in anticipation
I will make my way to heaven
lighthearted

Memorial Poems: A Collection of Poems Written in Tears

in memory of the countless souls who never found peace

1

this is a record of how
we crossed the border
like migratory birds,
who visit in the spring
and depart in the winter

famished, we flower swallows
roamed mountains and fields,
we crossed the border
to beg in a foreign nation

we harbored no ill will—
we were living off of grass porridge
everyone was hungry
there was no food to spare

we were more dead than alive
we are not to be blamed
rather than begging from those who have nothing
we crossed the border instead

2

how dare they brand us
outlaws, turncoats, and traitors
to the fatherland—
the country that bore and raised us

we were orphans
who had to leave the nation
in order to survive
we left in tears
to beg for food
we had no choice—
tell us: what crimes have we committed?

we are migratory birds
we took flight to survive
we are blameless, innocent
why do you insist
on charging us with high treason?

we inherited this hard life
from our parents
we have the right to value and protect
our lives
we are not traitors
rather, we are the heroes
of our time

3

yes—
we are the heroes of our time
I remember the pledge,
the solemn promise we made
to always offer one another
strength and courage
'

if I survive
I will write
about our struggle
it will be a heroic tale
a vivid story
about the heroes of our time

did you know
that we, too, are revolutionaries,
once we fought the Japanese
now, we fight in a desperate war
against death

we were too young
to face our enemies with guns
but the tale of our adventure
is about our battle with the grim reaper himself
is this not the true story of struggle?

4

we risked our lives
so many times
everyday we stood at the crossroads
between life and death
ragged, starving, and sick
so many swallows fell
like spring flowers

when will the world of our dreams
appear?
one free from cold and hunger
we countdown the days
we thirst for its arrival

all of you left me
before you could see the day
our small wish
our beautiful dream
came true

a warm cotton coat
a bowl of white rice
were these things too much to ask?
pipe dreams
harder to reach,
than a star in the night sky

5

every life is precious e
very person wants to live
but to live each day
in this unceasing hell
is all too exhausting

to end the suffering
members of our flock
chose death rather than life

a bird locked in a cage
without any food
will flap and struggle
and peck at the bars
until bright red blood
flows from its beak

the same is true of people
who died with their eyes wide open
while escaping this land shrouded in misery they
dreamed of life under a foreign sky
atop strange mountains and under distant waters
their calls for freedom resounding

6

kind, naive people
with hearts full of fire
who can console you?
who will unknot the anger and resentment
tangled deep within you?

worry not my determined friends
I will comfort and console you
I will step forth and celebrate you
I will tell the world your story

I will keep the promise we made that day
I will recall the days of suffering we endured
I will call to mind each of your faces
as I document your names in this book,
a record of our lives together

how we lived in poverty and destitution
how we endured hardships and loneliness
I was there with you through it all
who is better fit
to tell our story?

7

though you evaporated
like a drop of dew
nameless in a foreign land
you loved life with a fervor
yours, was a life of spark and flame

I remember you today
my friends
in those final, desperate moments
as you struggled to live
in spite of cold, hunger, and illness

I alone survived
and have become an adult
but I will never forget
the miserable sight
of you
taking your last breath

I feel an unbearable guilt
for being the only one
who did not die
I kneel before you and cry
I am sorry, my friends
forgive me, my friends!

8

I'm not an author or poet of any renown
I have no talent
I'm wholly unfit to write a book
but I write because I must
I write because I swore to you I would

how could I hesitate
or refuse to write my humble book
knowing that I might bring your souls some comfort
by informing the world
of our painful lives

I promised you I'd write a book
if I survived
so much time has passed
but I have kept my word

this collection
is soaked with my tears
I dedicate it to you:
my friends,
who lived short, difficult lives
O my friends, my brothers,
I miss and love you so

(written from a far off land)

Hyongrae Kim is a PhD Candidate in Comparative Literature at the University of Massachusetts Amherst, where he is conducting research on North Korean literary translation and interpreters in violent conflict situations. Kim has served as a linguistic specialist in various roles for the Republic of Korea.

Siobhan Meï is a PhD candidate in Comparative Literature at the University of Massachusetts Amherst, where she studies the intersections of feminism and translation. Her translations of poetry have appeared in *Asymptote, Transference,* and *carte blanche* among other places.

www.ingramcontent.com/pod-product-compliance
Lightning Source LLC
Chambersburg PA
CBHW061524020726
47502CB00006B/2226